LOVE

and other wars

Prachi Jha

BookLeaf Publishing

India | USA | UK

Copyright © Prachi Jha
All Rights Reserved.

This book has been self-published with all reasonable efforts taken to make the material error-free by the author. No part of this book shall be used, reproduced in any manner whatsoever without written permission from the author, except in the case of brief quotations embodied in critical articles and reviews.

The Author of this book is solely responsible and liable for its content including but not limited to the views, representations, descriptions, statements, information, opinions, and references ["Content"]. The Content of this book shall not constitute or be construed or deemed to reflect the opinion or expression of the Publisher or Editor. Neither the Publisher nor Editor endorse or approve the Content of this book or guarantee the reliability, accuracy, or completeness of the Content published herein and do not make any representations or warranties of any kind, express or implied, including but not limited to the implied warranties of merchantability, fitness for a particular purpose.

The Publisher and Editor shall not be liable whatsoever...

Made with ❤ on the BookLeaf Publishing Platform
www.bookleafpub.in
www.bookleafpub.com

Dedication

To Neelima Jha aka mummy,
To Narendra Kumar Jha aka papa, and
To Pratyush Jha aka Brother Dear...

Through every high and every low,
You have been the roots that helped me grow.
If words could measure all that for me you do,
This book would be but page 1 of my Thank you.

Preface

It all began in 7th grade. As a bright student, I was asked to write an article or a poem on Gandhiji for Gandhi Jayanti. But, in the rush of schoolwork, I had completely forgotten about it. On the morning of the submission, as I stood at the bus stop, panic set in. I turned to my mother and asked, "What do I do now?" She handed me an old school magazine with an article on Gandhiji and said, "Take inspiration from this and write a poem."
Both her and I still remember the exact words I said in response, "Poem?! I am not a lyricist or anything. How will I write a poem?"
She simply smiled and said, "Then don't. Just write a paragraph. Take inspiration and write anything."

I nodded, got into the bus, and reached school. I sat down, intending to write an article. But somewhere in that moment, something shifted, I tried rhyming a few words, and suddenly, the lines started flowing effortlessly. I was surprised at how naturally they came to me. When I submitted my poem, my teacher was also impressed. And that was it, the beginning of something I never saw coming.

Hundreds of poems later, I still remember the day my

college professor called me a **"poem machine"**—she said, "Give her a topic, and a poem will come out on the other side. She can write about anything under the sun."

From my mother's unwitting push to what has become a lifelong love for poetry, this journey has been incredible; and now, finally putting my work into this anthology, I feel an overwhelming mix of joy, nostalgia, and gratitude.

I hope you enjoy reading these poems as much as I loved writing them. And if you do, maybe, just maybe, it will inspire me to write even more.

P.S.: That first-ever poem on Gandhiji was published in our school newsletter. But in my excitement, I never saved a copy—something my mother still scolds me for to this day! So, here you go, Mumma—a hard copy of many of my poems, for you to keep safely.

See you in the books!

Acknowledgements

Writing this poetry collection has been an incredible journey, and I wouldn't have completed it without the unwavering support of so many wonderful people.

First and foremost, my heartfelt gratitude to BookLeaf Publishing for making this process so seamless and approachable. Their initiative is truly a game-changer for aspiring writers like me, especially for those who feel lost in the world of publishing. The affordability, the simplicity, and the sheer encouragement they provide were exactly the push I needed to get back to writing.

My parents, who have always supported my goals, and have always pushed me to do great at any and every co-curricular activity. (After I have aced academically of course! XD)

My brother, whose love for all things unique has always nudged me toward "the road less traveled". Yet, paradoxically, he was also the biggest force behind me becoming an IIM alumnus. Go figure XD

To Salomika, who stayed up late with me, helping me create (or just choose XD) the best cover for this book, from the 100s that we looked at. I am very happy with my "choice". I am also indebted to you for all the hard work that you have put in creating this book's cover!

To all my friends, who insisted I put my poetry out into the world, starting with college bulletin boards and eventually, my Instagram handle. From gifting me poetry books in every possible language to fueling the dream that maybe, just maybe, I'd become rich enough to fund our annual vacations XD

Jokes apart, this book is for everyone who has ever showed any trust in my extremely procrastinated and laidback process.

From Akriti (bhabhi) always telling my parents, "You have put her in the wrong field, she is meant for something creative!" to my best friend Arundhati, encouraging me to write since standard 10th, when I was writing meaningless novels day in, day out. From Aditi lending her beautiful art as background for all my poems put up on the college bulletin board to Anu, Salomika and Aru, whose birthday gifts were always poetry books, paired with relentless requests (read: demands) for me to write more. From Vasu standing tall with his "I will support you if you want to do an MA, a PhD in English", to Vishi di's "You are like a different person when you write!". From Riddhi's and Anya's amazing encouragement to me being "If you can't write on anything, write on me, write on how good I am", to Ash bhai going all "You are worth more than you take credit for". From Puru bombarding me with Eminem reels to help me grasp the art of double entendre to Rishi getting me out of my lockdown "writer's block" with words of encouragement.

From my teachers in school, to my faculty in college... Every person who has encouraged me to write more!

And finally, this book is for **you**, the reader. If a self-proclaimed lazy procrastinator like me can make this happen, trust me—you can too.

Aim for the stars,
For even if you fall short,
You'll land on the moon.

1. Yours Truly

I am a better version of myself,
Without you.
So, they say.
You are so much better...
We like you this way!

But would you like me?
Without you...
Without your thoughts,
Not just you on my mind.
Not thinking of you, all the time?

I think you would not.
But how would you know?
Did you ever see That version of me?
That I really don't show
To you, to a friend, or a foe.

The version where I am both fire and ice.
I burn.
I suffice.
I am the best version of both.
But not the version you would like.

Still, if you were to inquire,
What would my favorite version be,
Of me?
I'd just smile and fire...
"Yours".

2. I know, you know

I know this:
I love you,
You love you.
It's a one-way street,
I will still walk through!

I know this:
It's a little unfair,
I love your eyes, your hair.
But about my smile,
Do you even care?

I know this:
You can deceive me, lie.
I'll laugh it off, or maybe cry,
But won't gather the courage,
To just ask you... Why?!

You should know this:
I still hold you dear,
Whether you are far or near.
And if this road doesn't lead to you,
It is taking me nowhere...

3. Broken Hearts

Only a broken heart bleeds,
It is said.
Only a broken heart can sing.
And unlike the myth of true love,
A broken heart is a real thing!

It breaks you open,
Bone by bone.
And rips apart each nerve.
But I have heard it's Karma's game,
Serving you what you deserve.

What goes around comes back,
As you sowed,
So will you reap.
You can't outrun a broken heart,
When it's your turn to weep!

But you can mend a broken heart,
I believe.
If you give it time to heal,
And when Karma's work is done,
Of whatever you were meant to feel.

4. What is it all about

It is not always about,
A yes or a no...
Or whether really,
To stay or to go...

Neither is it,
As easy as ABC,
Nor is it about,
To be or not to be!

Its more about,
That turmoil in your head,
That tear stained pillow,
Lying by your bed.

It's about that smile,
That faded without a word.
But it was,
Just a name that you heard!

The distant memory,
Still fresh in your mind,
Because you believed it was,
One of a kind!

And why?
Why does it all,
Still knock the air out.
Because truly,
This is what it is all about…

5. Gold and Sand

Once you catch hold,
Of the moon!
Does its brilliance diminish,
Just as soon?

I looked from afar,
And I saw a mirage of gold...
Once I held it in my hand,
It felt like sand...
Or so I was told?

Once I reached my destination,
Now I miss the road!
The shiny thing that kept me awake,
All night...
Now seems too old...

I got what I wanted,
But my passion now seems lost,
I have captured the light in my fist,
But... At what cost?

I have all that I wanted,
But I am still ill at ease...

Was it really sand not gold,
That had brought me all the peace. ...

6. Unspoken words

I remember the first time,
That you held my hand,
I had butterflies, but I looked away,
Did you understand?

My eyes still search for you,
Somedays you also look and smile…
But if I am being honest to myself,
Its's been a while.

A while to our shared laughter,
A while to our trips,
A while to the hours of hand holding,
A while since we brushed our lips.

Our paths still cross in lonely lobbies,
And sometimes in vacant cabins,
But I can't see those days in your eyes,
To you, were they guilty sins?!

I will never have the courage to ask you,
These answers might never be heard…
But wouldn't it all have been better,
Had you just read, my unspoken words!

7. Distance makes the heart grow fonder?

It has been months and months,
Since I last saw a glimpse of you,
The sun doesn't shine as bright,
Even the clouds are feeling blue!

The last time that we met,
Our hands and hearts intertwined,
But that must have been ages ago,
When the right stars had aligned!

To see you smile outside the screen,
Is a joy I can't put in words,
But now that you are back in there,
All of this just seems absurd!

You are my go-to person,
For every news good and bad,
But pouring my heart to a computer screen,
Sometimes becomes a tad bit too sad!

Distance makes the heart go fonder,
Or so it is said,

I think you would also agree to disagree,
When you'll lie down alone in a bed!

8. People ruin beautiful things

Not long ago I read,
A thought-provoking quote,
That said:
Keep a secret, all of your being,
Because people ruin beautiful things...

Keep that win a secret, it said.
Take your victory, to your solitary bed,
The envious they are, the happier they appear...
To be honest, they don't really care.
So unaccompanied,
Just focus on the joy this success brings,
Because people ruin beautiful things...

Kiss and tell no one, it said.
Take all your love to your solitary bed,
They'll judge and question and cut and peel,
From them, it's "tea"; Not how you "feel",
So just silently listen to the song your heart sings,
Because people ruin beautiful things...

So, take it all to your solitary bed,
Your pain, sorrow, sadness, pain and tears,

You hope, peace, and love...
Everything you hold dear!
But never let their envy, do your decision making,
Because...

9. Masterpiece

Should my masterpiece be the end of me?
This question perennially gnaws at my mind,
Should your masterpiece be the end of you?
I believe that's what we are all here to find...

A masterpiece is a person's greatest piece of work.
It's supposed to showcase an outstanding amount of skill set,
But 'Who' decides for me 'What' my masterpiece is?
Will it be me, my loved ones, or someone I haven't even met!

'Who' decides 'When' will my masterpiece be...
Do I get to do it, by my own sheer will?
Or will the crowd that I stand in decides,
That it can only happen, when my time stands still!

'Who' decides 'Where' will my masterpiece be...
Will it rest peacefully beside the Bay of Naples?
Or will it be painted outside Johnsy's window,
Being told for centuries as part of fables?

'Who' decides 'How' will my masterpiece be...
Will it be about earning the most amount of money?

Or will it be beyond these earthly possessions,
Propelling the viewer into a retrospective journey!

All of these myriad questions have left me with a 'Why'?
Why should my masterpiece be reflective of my end?
Why can't it be my start, my beginning?
And every broken piece that my art will mend!

10. Pause and Breathe

In this life of hustle,
Day in, day out...
We chase and we run,
But forget what it's all about.

I prayed for this door to open,
Knocked on it day and night,
Now I walk right through it,
Yet don't glance back—right?

I'm living today,
At least one answered prayer,
But no time to pause,
As the next problem
Already meets my stare!

Take a halt,
Breathe it in, my friend.
Say your thank-you,
Show your grace—
This is not the end.

11. It does get better

Dark clouds do give way,
To Rainbows by the bay...
All you have to do my darling,
Is look the other way!

Give up trying to find,
Something so eternally divine,
In this pit of forever disappoint.
For once, let your heart lose to your mind!

Because this brilliant mind knows,
That this lonely heart will grow,
When it won't have to endlessly wait,
For fulfilment of promises hollow!

And once you are on the other side,
You will finally see in the daylight,
Just how happy you can be,
Oh, my Dear, how you've survived!

So let go of the" I wish I was her",
Don't cling to those meaningless letters,
Just take my word for it darling,
It does get BETTER!

12. Cost of life

Why is the voice inside my head,
Never at rest...
And why do I always want to attain,
The best of the best?!

Don't you have all you wished for?
Well one could always want more!
There is no peace if all you think is:
There could be more in store...

Well, what's the worst than can happen?
The wildest nightmare of men?
That no matter how much of it you have,
Happiness can't be bought by Yen!

What else can these Dollars then buy?
Oh, anything else you can try,
But they sadly also won't be your company,
When you, well, eventually die!

13. Lazy mornings

I slowly open one eye,
Stretching, preparing to wake up.
Warm blanket, cool breeze of air.
Oh, it is the perfect Sunday setup!

I push myself out of the bed,
And to the kitchen I go.
Where I put my glass full of water,
On the stove gas's burning glow!

With a cute little mug in hand,
I make it to the balcony somehow,
My path being intercepted,
By small paws and cute meows!

I sit down on my swing,
With soft fur touching my feet,
The warm sunlight falls on my face,
While the cool air brushes my cheeks!

I am alone with my thoughts,
Perhaps the only time of the day,
When I can sit quietly for hours,
Nothing to do or say!

Oh, how blessed it is to absorb,
All the warmth this brings.
At last, the corporate slave understands,
The beauty of lazy mornings!

14. Child marriage

Once upon a time,
In a village as beautiful as art,
Lived 2 best friends,
Let's hear their story from the start.

The first girl was from a progressive family,
Taara was her name.
She was 12, and dreamt to be a doctor,
To end the villager's pain.

The second girl was from a regressive family,
Maala was her name,
She was 12, and dreamt to be married,
Because to have any other dream would be insane!

Taara finished her schooling,
And her parents sent her off to college,
Whereas Maala's parents began preparation,
To arrange the grandest wedding of the village.

Taara studied hard day and night,
To realize her dream of being a doctor,
Whereas Maala, already married at 16,
Was ready to hear her first child's laughter!

Taara had finally become a pulmonologist,
A specialist of conditions of the lung,
But she returned home to find Maala very sick,
Because of having her pregnancy so young!

Taara was devastated,
And tried hard to save her sick friend,
But however hard she tried,
She couldn't save her in the end!

All because of her parents' negligence,
Of marrying her off at such a young age,
Taara lost her best friend Maala,
And now she wanted to leave this cage!

Taara and her family finally left the village,
Because they had understood,
The perils of evils like child marriage!
It should be ended for good!

15. It's not the butterflies

It's not when your heart races,
It's not when your hands shake,
It's not when your brain is moving so fast,
You think it would just break!

It's not when you are oh so nervous,
It's not when your feet go cold,
All of it is part of the lies,
Which from centuries we are told!

That our knight in shining armor,
Would give us butterflies in our stomach.
But how would you know this is a lie?!
You are so caught up with your butterfly.

That quite fleeting gaze across the room,
Which you don't notice, you disregard.
That is what it is,
And not from now, from the start!

How at peace you feel,
There is no euphoria in the air,
Just you, and this peace and this calm,
But about this you don't care?!

You run after what is unrequited,
The roller coaster of lows and highs.
Happy with those counted days of laughter,
In a sea of pain, sadness and deep sighs!

Your Paradise is right around the around,
But you are just letting is pass you by...
Someday you'll see, how happy you can be,
When you'll stop chasing those butterflies!

16. Love is... scary

I had a blind date planned,
Nervous as I was.
Got ready in a jiffy,
There was no time to pause!

I got a call from her suddenly,
"There is a last-minute change in plan",
The venue is now in a new place,
But I agreed, since I am a "green flag man"!

This place looked really desolate,
Looked a lot like an old construction site,
Then she walked towards me from far,
She looked so ethereal in white!

I asked about her change in plans,
She smiled a little, her cheeks red,
"You know how it is with Mumbai constructions."
I nodded, agreeing with all she said.

"It's been such a menace lately", I added.
"Do you know how many lives are lost?"
She asked this with such a straight face,
I lost my chain of thoughts.

Just then my phone rang loud,
I was shocked to see it was her call!
"Hey this is M's friend; she has met with an accident..."
My brain couldn't take this at all!

I looked at the girl Infront of me,
"Who are you?! Man, you lied?!"
It been so lonely for me here, she said.
And I wanted you to see, where I died!

17. Tiny wisdom

I look outside my window,
There I see a gloomy grey cat,
Reflecting my gloom more or less.
Let's leave it at that.

I look at my watch,
Oh, I am already late for office!
Why do bad thing happen to me,
That's what my first thought is.

Everywhere I see,
There is one or more problem around,
Now there is the loud noise from outside,
Oh, I will go crazy with that sound!

Just then a little bird came through my window,
And sat quietly on my hand...
It wasn't able to fly properly,
Its wings covered in wet sand!

Still the bird was trying its best,
Looking at me with its little hopeful eyes,
And suddenly this little bird's beating heart,
Had taken over my depressed sighs!

I tried to help the little birdy out,
Brushing its wings lightly, one by one.
And before I could give up on it,
All the cleaning work was done!

The bird was happy and chirping again,
Showing no sign of adversity,
Made me self-reflect in no time,
If I should get out of my pit of self-pity!

Learning from this little birdy,
How it was chirping through the toil,
Along with helping me save myself,
From this day I had plans to spoil!

18. Hopelessly... In love

You are what comes to my mind,
When I envisage a perfect human being.
You see the Whole wide world
Then why is it just You, I am seeing...

I talk to myself for hours straight,
You just nod your head and smile,
You say, " Oh God it has been hours",
But to me, it feels like it's only been a while!

I say a lot of things I shouldn't,
You stay quiet about the things said,
You say, you see the world in all the Rainbow colors,
Then why is it that, all I see is RED!

I think about dinners with you,
Us, talking endlessly about food,
And to be completely honest,
Your mention itself brightens up my mood!

I've finally reached a conclusion,
I guess it's a crazy co-incidence or two,
You are in love with your own great self, and,
I'm hopelessly in love with YOU!

19. Excuse me... not

I'll do it when the rainy season ends,
I'll do it when it stops being so cold...
Don't these lines sound like excuses,
To your own self you have told?

I am waiting for the right moment,
I am waiting for the perfect start.
Making best out of a bad moment,
Is the real skill, the real art!

That bestseller novelist began writing,
As a single mother with no money.
So go out now, toil in the rain,
Stop waiting for it to be sunny!

Stop listening to those baseless excuses,
Just listen to your heart's desire!
Because destiny really does favors those,
Who work the hardest, in the fire!

20. History of... Love

Romeo and Juliet embraced death for each other,
For Antony and Cleopatra, it was love at first sight,
Layla and Majnu were united only in death,
and not any different was Heer and Ranjha's plight.

Helenna and Paris's affection led to the Trojan war,
Whereas Shah Jahan and Mumtaz gave us the monument
of love,
Lancelot and Guinevere led to the division of the 'Round
Table',
For Orpheus and Eurydice one life wasn't enough.

These stories make us stop and wonder,
What these lovers had known all along,
That true LOVE between two souls,
Has the power to prove the whole world wrong!

21. This one is for you

Dear... You,
Don't give up on love, altogether,
If you got your heart broken once...
Well, if you get run out in a cricket match,
Will you completely give up on scoring runs?!

No, you won't, rather you'd strive harder next time,
Because last time, just wasn't enough...
Well then why should the rules be different,
For this never-ending game of LOVE?

Well, in this game of Hearts,
While someone wins, someone definitely loses,
It's like creating a garden full of thorned roses,
So, my dear, be ready for the bruises!

So, you,
Don't give up altogether on LOVE,
Just because HE broke your heart...
Pick up the broken pieces and sew them together,
Because every full stop, can blossom into a Fresh Start!

www.ingramcontent.com/pod-product-compliance
Lightning Source LLC
La Vergne TN
LVHW010830200726
843508LV00012B/2544